Aa is for Angela Angel

Instructions

1. Trace all the dotted letters.
2. Find and circle the initial sound in each word.
3. Colour the angel.
4. Cut out on the dotted lines.
6. Attach string to the top.
7. Staple dress at the back.
8. Slide the head section into the dress to make Angela.

ⓐpple

alligator

angel

Angela

Prim-Ed Publishing

1

Initial Sounds Through Art and Craft — Book 2

Fully Reproducible Copymasters

LOWER

INITIAL SOUNDS
THROUGH
ART AND CRAFT 2

by Helen Hall

COPYRIGHT INFORMATION
This master may only be reproduced by the original purchaser for use with their class(es). The publisher prohibits the loaning or onselling of this master for purposes of reproduction.

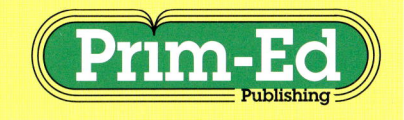

ISBN 1-86400-464-9

Prim-Ed Publishing

Initial Sounds through Art and Craft – Book 2
Prim-Ed Publishing

First published in 1998 by R.I.C. Publications
Reprinted under license in 1998 by Prim-Ed Publishing

Copyright Helen Hall 1998

This master may only be reproduced by the original
purchaser for use with their class(es) only.
The publisher prohibits the loaning or onselling of
this master for the purposes of reproduction.

ISBN 1 86400 464 9
PR–0996

Additional title available in this series:
Initial Sounds through Art and Craft – Book 1

Prim-Ed Publishing Pty. Ltd.
Offices in: United Kingdom: PO Box 051, Nuneaton, Warwickshire, CV11 6ZU
Australia: PO Box 332, Greenwood, Western Australia, 6024
Republic of Ireland: PO Box 8, New Ross, County Wexford, Ireland

Copyright Notice

Blackline masters or copy masters are published and sold with a limited copyright. This copyright allows publishers to provide teachers and schools with a wide range of learning activities without copyright being breached. This limited copyright allows the purchaser to make sufficient copies for use within their own education institution. The copyright is not transferable, nor can it be onsold. Following these instructions is not essential but will ensure that you, as the purchaser, have evidence of legal ownership to the copyright if inspection occurs.
For your added protection in the case of copyright inspection, please complete the form below. Retain this form, the complete original document and the invoice or receipt as proof of purchase.

Name of Purchaser:_____   Date of Purchase:_____

Supplier:_____   School Order#(if applicable):_____

Signature of Purchaser:_____

INITIAL SOUNDS THROUGH ART AND CRAFT 2

Written by Helen Hall
Published by Prim-Ed Publishing

Foreword

Initial Sounds Through Art and Craft – Book 1 has been such a success with lower primary teachers we have released a second book! *Initial Sounds Through Art and Craft – Book 2* is designed to introduce and reinforce the learning of initial single sounds in the first weeks at school.

Each page contains a different activity designed to be motivational and fun. Clear directions are included on each page which require pupils to practise manipulative skills such as cutting, colouring, gluing and folding. These activities have been tried and tested in the early years with great success.

Using the Worksheets

Clear directions are provided and can be read aloud and discussed.

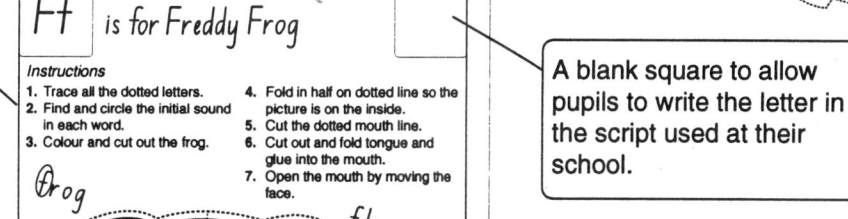

A blank square to allow pupils to write the letter in the script used at their school.

Pupils follow directions to construct the activity.

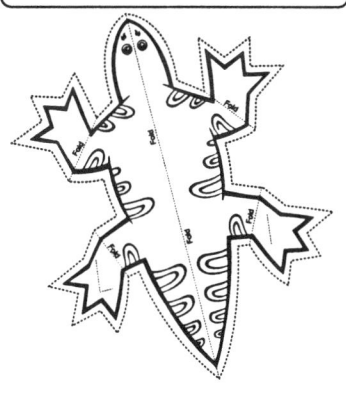

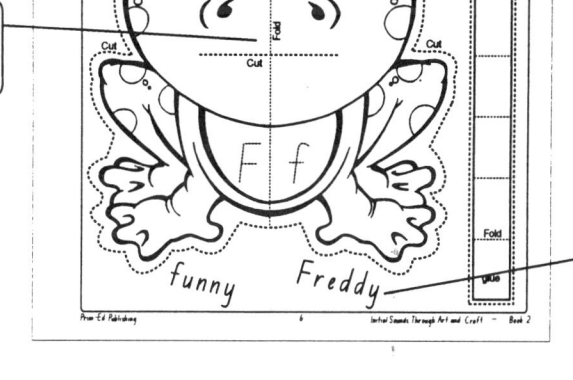

Pupils find and identify the initial sound in words placed in the page.

Teaching Suggestions

- For best results, photocopying each activity onto light card.
- Activities can be enlarged to A3 size.
- Introduce sounds by:
  - using repetitive rhymes or songs;
  - making letters from modelling clay;
  - tracing letters in sand or finger paint; or
  - finding objects or words with the initial sound in the classroom or outside.
- Use the art and craft activity as the basis for writing.

Prim-Ed Publishing i Initial Sounds Through Art and Craft – Book 2

Bb is for bouncing bird

Instructions

1. Trace all the dotted letters.
2. Find and circle the initial sound in each word.
3. Colour the bird and wings.
4. Cut out the wings and body on the dotted lines.
5. Slide the wings into the body.
6. Fold the wings back on the dotted lines
7. Attach string to bird.

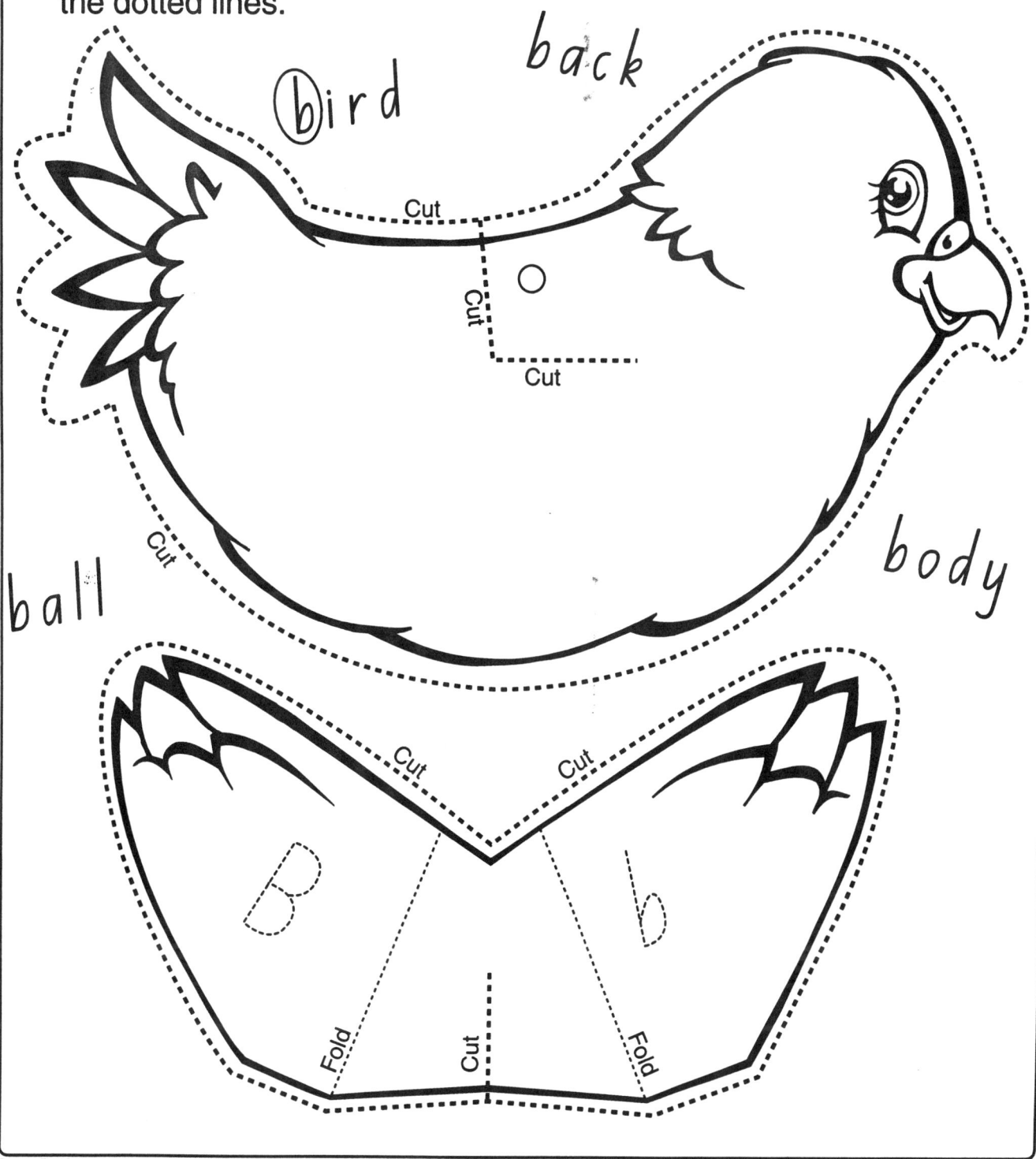

bird

back

ball

body

Prim-Ed Publishing 2 Initial Sounds Through Art and Craft — Book 2

Cc is for colourful clown

Instructions

1. Trace all the dotted letters.
2. Find and circle the initial sound in each word.
3. Colour the clown.
4. Cut out the clown on the dotted lines.
5. Carefully cut out the eye holes.
6. Attach string to each side.

ⓒlown

can

cat

car

Cut

Cut

Dd is for dancing duck

Instructions

1. Trace all the dotted letters.
2. Find and circle the initial sound in each word.
3. Colour the duck and the dancing feet.
4. Cut out the circle.
5. Attach the circle behind the duck with a split pin.
6. Spin the wheel to see the dancing duck.

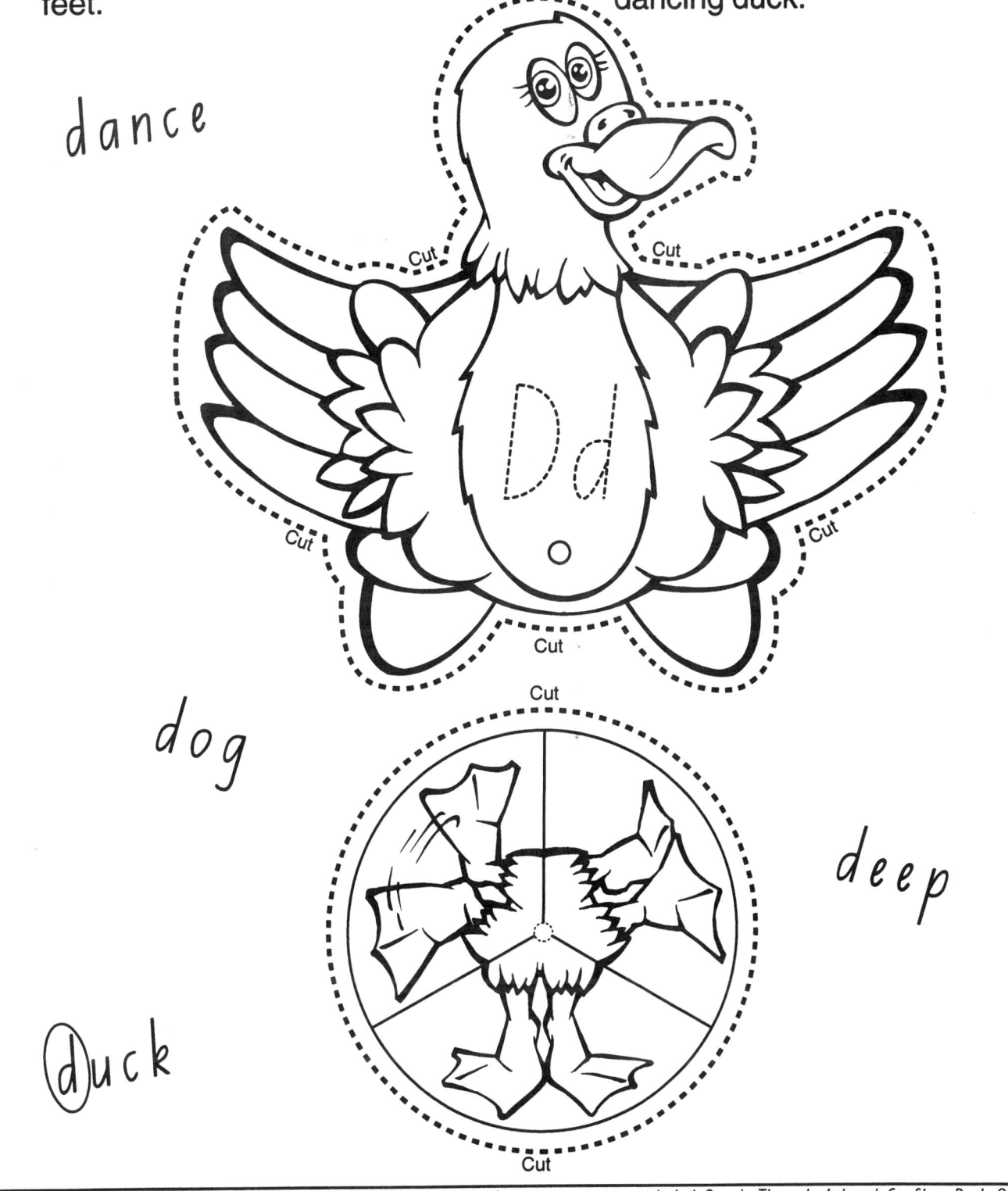

dance

dog

deep

ⓓuck

Prim-Ed Publishing

4

Initial Sounds Through Art and Craft – Book 2

Ee is for Elly Elephant

Instructions

1. Trace all the dotted letters.
2. Find and circle the initial sound in each word.
3. Cut out the rectangle.
4. Fold in half.
5. Colour Elly.
6. Cut out Elly around the dotted line.
7. Push the head down carefully in the direction of the arrow.
8. Fold the trunk like a concertina.

eagle

Easter

egg

elephant   Elly   emu

Prim-Ed Publishing — Initial Sounds Through Art and Craft – Book 2

Ff is for Freddy Frog

Instructions

1. Trace all the dotted letters.
2. Find and circle the initial sound in each word.
3. Colour and cut out the frog.
4. Fold in half on dotted line so the picture is on the inside.
5. Cut the dotted mouth line.
6. Cut out and fold tongue and glue into the mouth.
7. Open the mouth by moving the face.

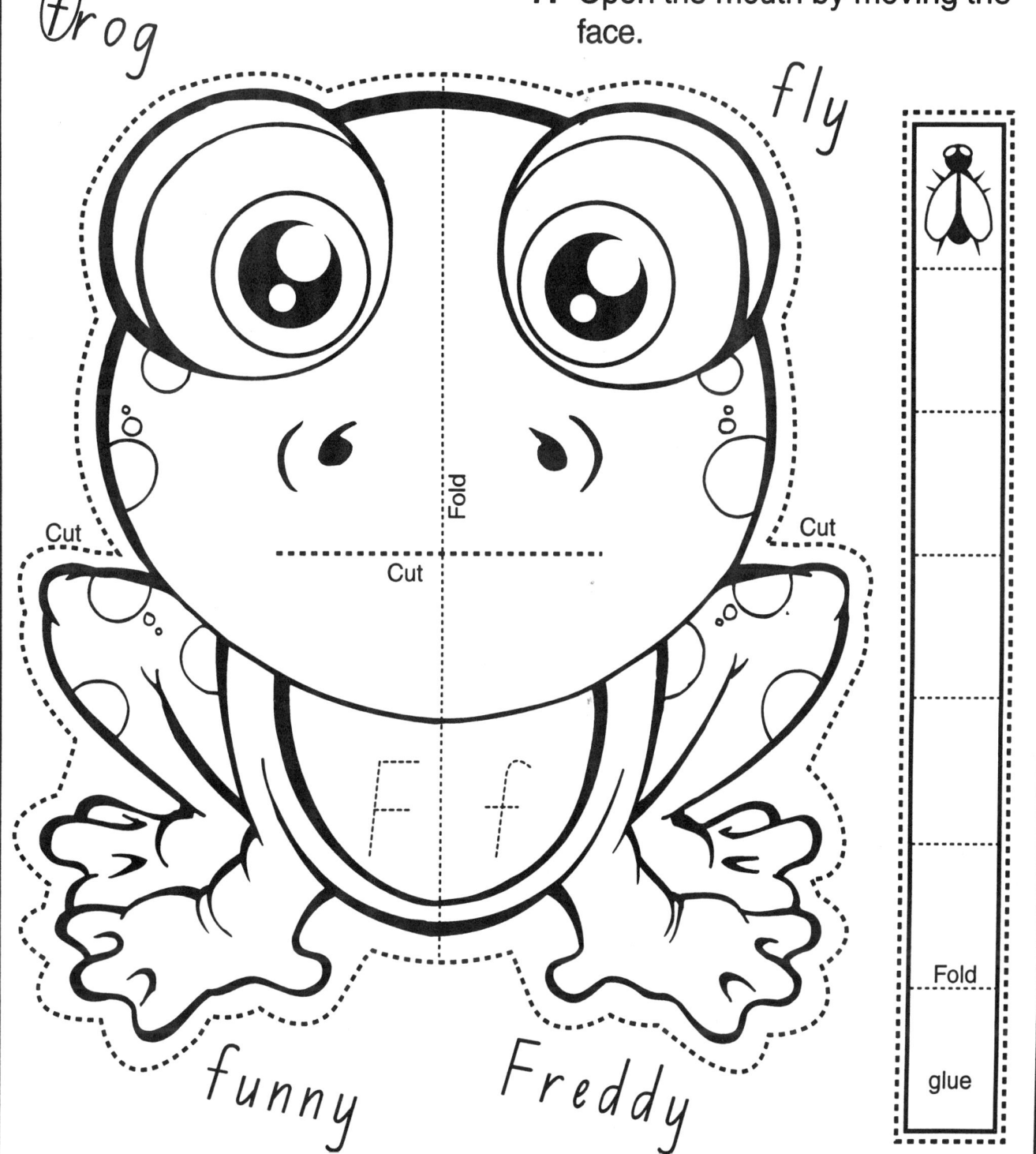

frog

fly

Cut

Fold

Cut

Cut

Ff

funny

Freddy

Fold

glue

Prim-Ed Publishing

Initial Sounds Through Art and Craft — Book 2

Gg is for green ghost

Instructions

1. Trace all the dotted letters.
2. Find and circle the initial sound in each word.
3. Colour the ghost green.
4. Cut out the rectangle.
5. Fold in half with the picture on the outside.
6. Glue along the inside side edges.
7. Cut out around the bottom of the ghost on the dotted line.
8. Put your fingers inside the ghost's body to fly your ghost puppet.

Edge

Edge

Fold

ⓖhost

green

go

goat

get

gorilla

girl

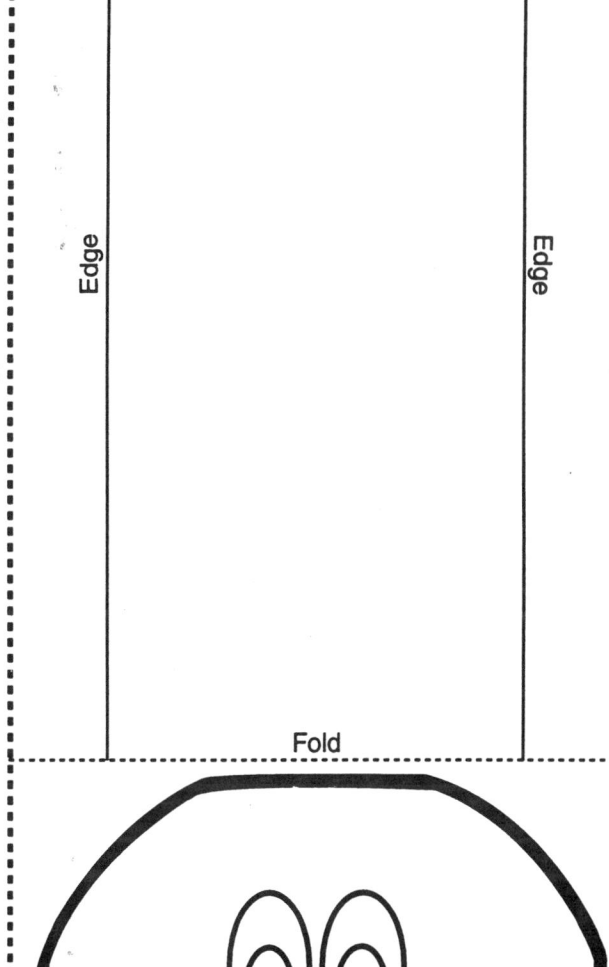

Prim-Ed Publishing

Initial Sounds Through Art and Craft — Book 2

Hh is for hovering helicopter

Instructions

1. Trace all the dotted letters.
2. Find and circle the initial sound in each word.
3. Cut out the helicopter along the bold lines.
4. Fold on dotted lines as shown.
5. Attach a paperclip to the bottom.
6. Drop from a height.

(h)elicopter

house

hat

horse

hello

Harry

Ii is for Impy Indian

Instructions

1. Trace all the dotted letters.
2. Find and circle the initial sound in each word.
3. Colour and cut out the headband.
4. Cut a long strip of paper to fit the child's head.
5. Glue the band to the longer strip of paper and staple to fit.

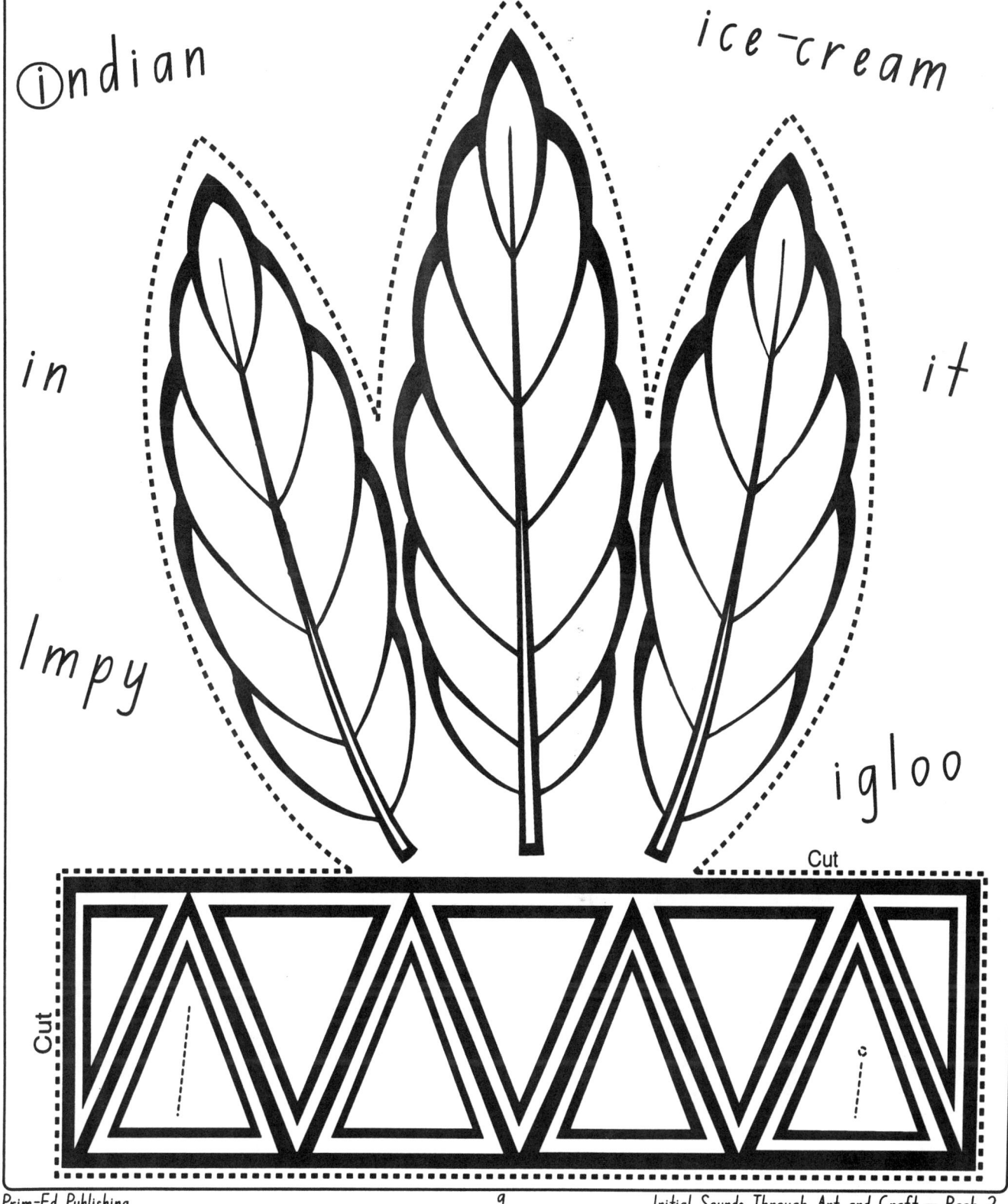

ⓘndian

ice-cream

in

it

Impy

igloo

Cut

Cut

Jj is for Jumping Jack

Instructions

1. Trace all the letters.
2. Find and circle the initial sound in each word.
3. Colour the letter 'j' on the box.
4. Cut out the box.
5. Colour and cut out Jack and the strip.
6. Fold the strip into a concertina.
7. Glue one end of the strip to the top of the box.
8. Glue the other end of the strip to the bottom of the Jack's head.

jetty

jump

jelly

Prim-Ed Publishing — Initial Sounds Through Art and Craft – Book 2

Kk is for Kirsty Koala

Instructions

1. Trace all the dotted letters.
2. Find and circle the initial sound in each word.
3. Colour and cut out the koala pieces.
4. Fold rectangle in half with picture on the outside.
5. Glue along inside edges.
7. Glue on koala's head.
8. Put your fingers inside the koala's body to make a puppet.

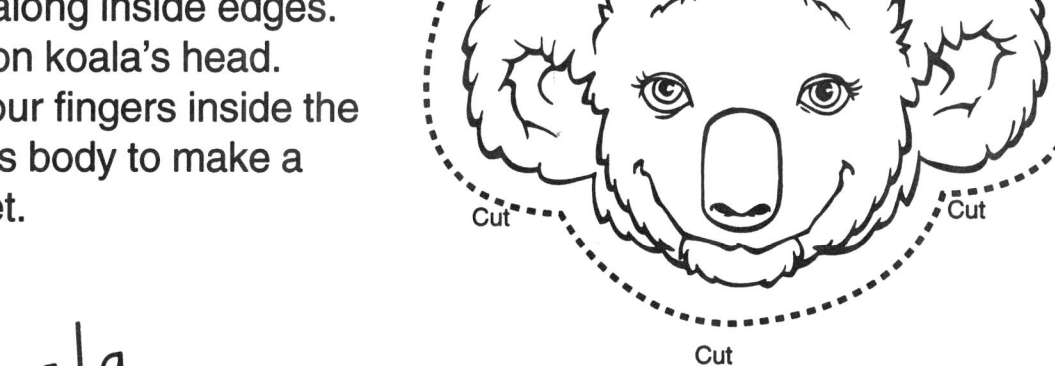

koala

kangaroo

king

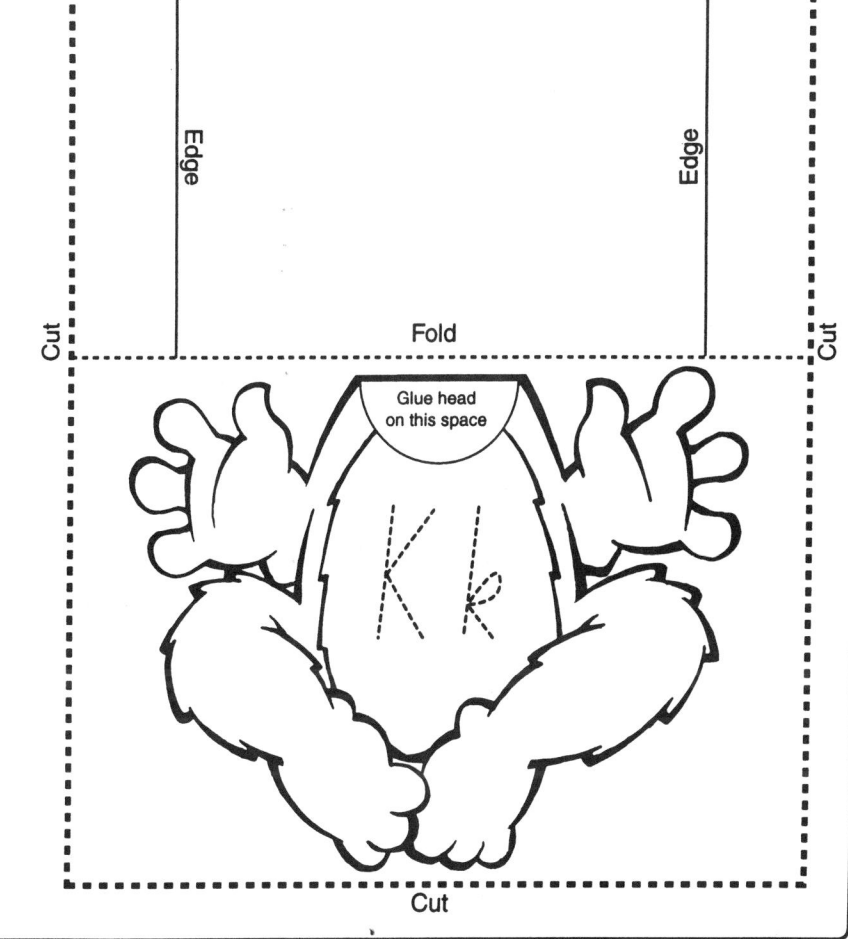

Cut
Cut
Cut
Cut
Edge
Edge
Fold
Cut
Cut
Glue head on this space
Kk

Prim-Ed Publishing   Initial Sounds Through Art and Craft – Book 2

Ll is for leaping lizard

Instructions

1. Trace all the dotted letters.
2. Find and circle the initial sound in each word.
3. Colour and cut out the lizard.
4. Fold in half along dotted line.
5. Fold the legs as shown.

lizard

little

lazy

lion

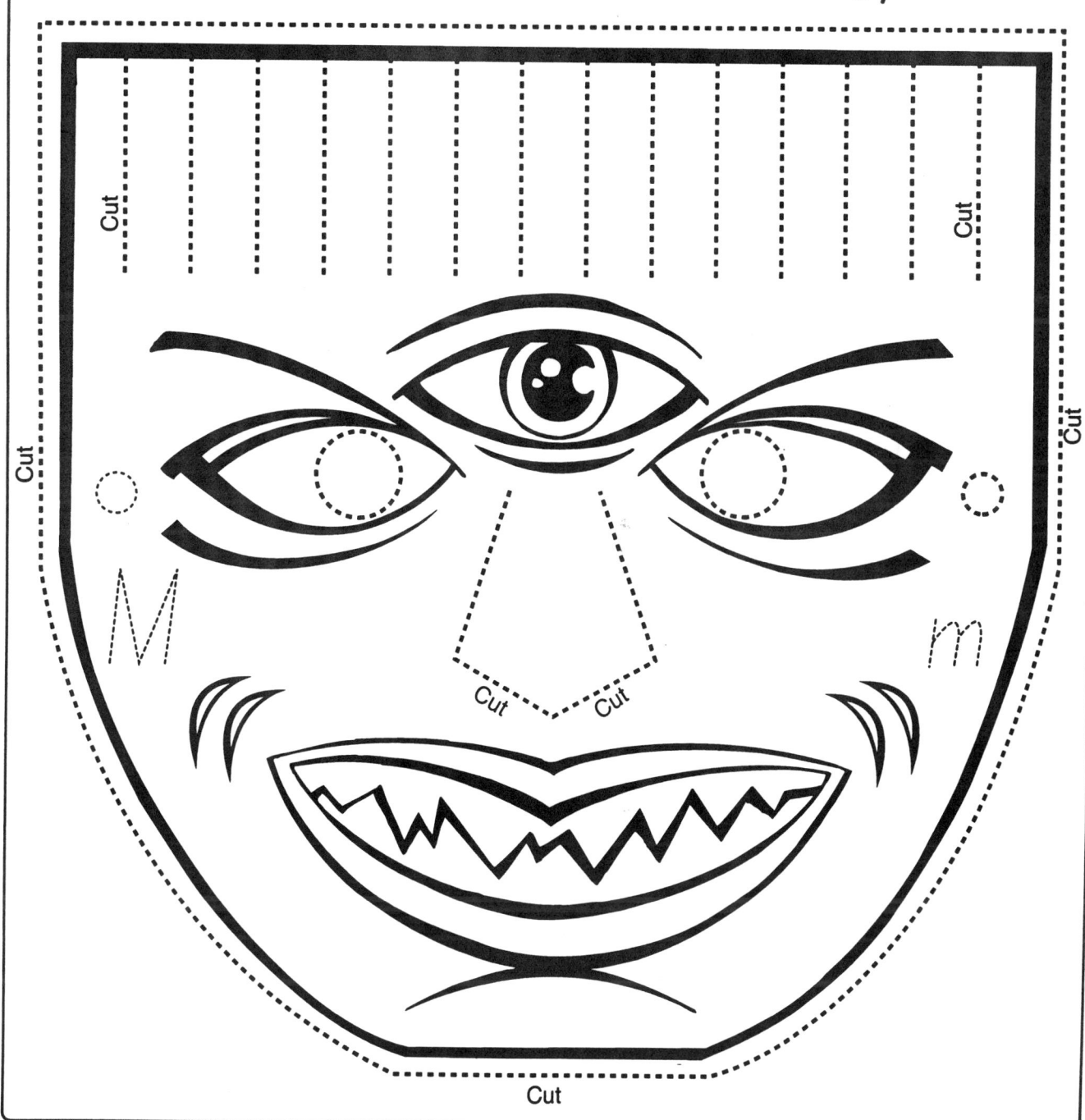

Mm is for monster mask

Instructions

1. Trace all the dotted letters.
2. Find and circle the initial sound in each word.
3. Colour and cut out the mask.
4. Cut lines to form hair.
5. Curl the hair with a pencil.
6. Carefully cut and fold the nose forward.
7. Carefully cut holes for the eyes.

mask   mouse   monster

Prim-Ed Publishing　　　　13　　　　Initial Sounds Through Art and Craft – Book 2

Nn is for nifty noodles

Instructions

1. Trace all the dotted letters.
2. Find and circle the initial sound in each word.
3. Colour and cut out noodles.
4. Colour and cut out bowl.
5. Curl the noodles with a pencil.
6. Glue the noodles onto the bowl.

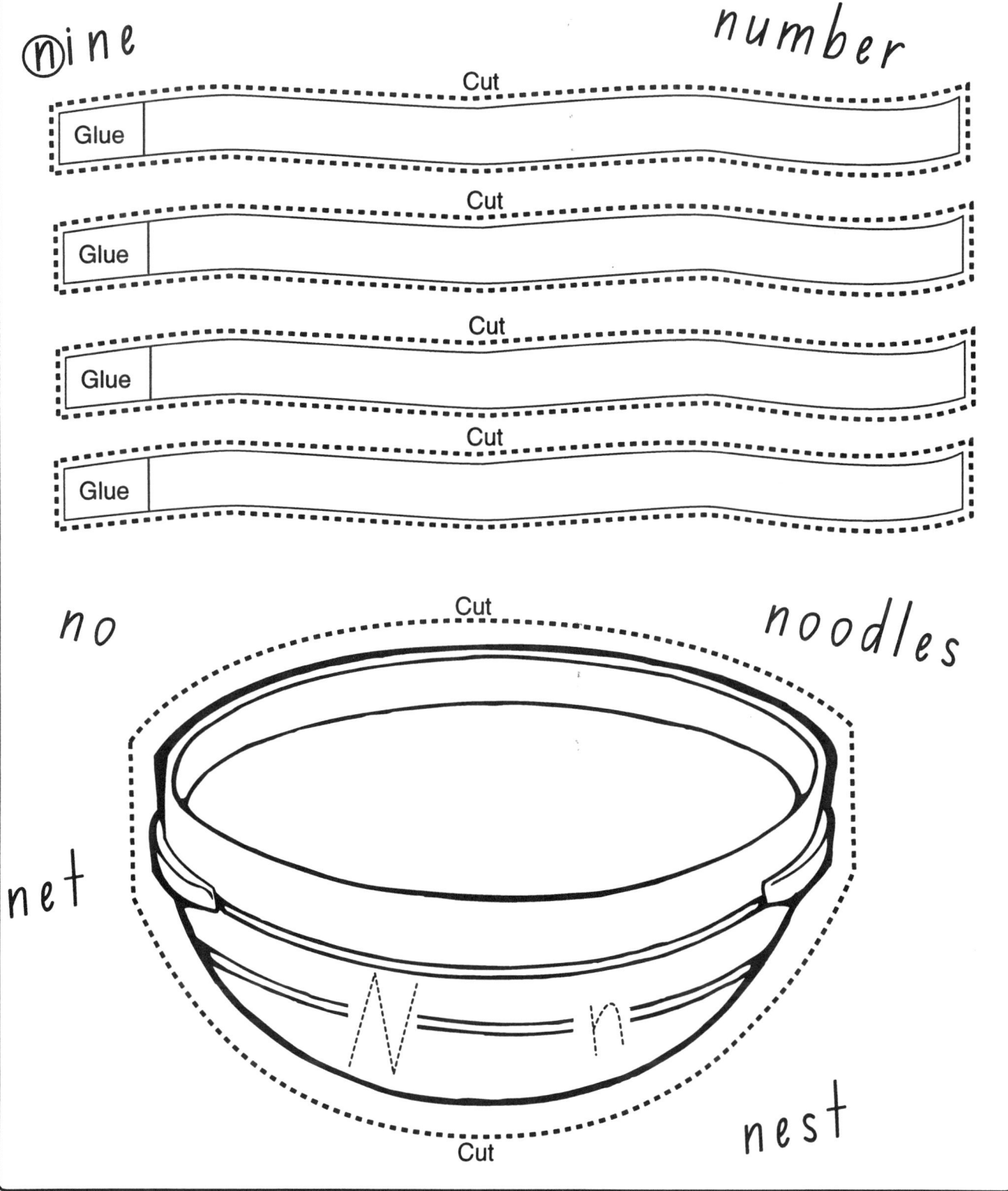

(n)ine   number

no   noodles

net   nest

Oo is for origami owl

Instructions

1. Trace all the dotted letters.
2. Find and circle the initial sound in each word.
3. Colour the owl's wings and body.
4. Cut out the owl.
5. Turn the owl on its back and fold along the dotted lines so it can sit forward.

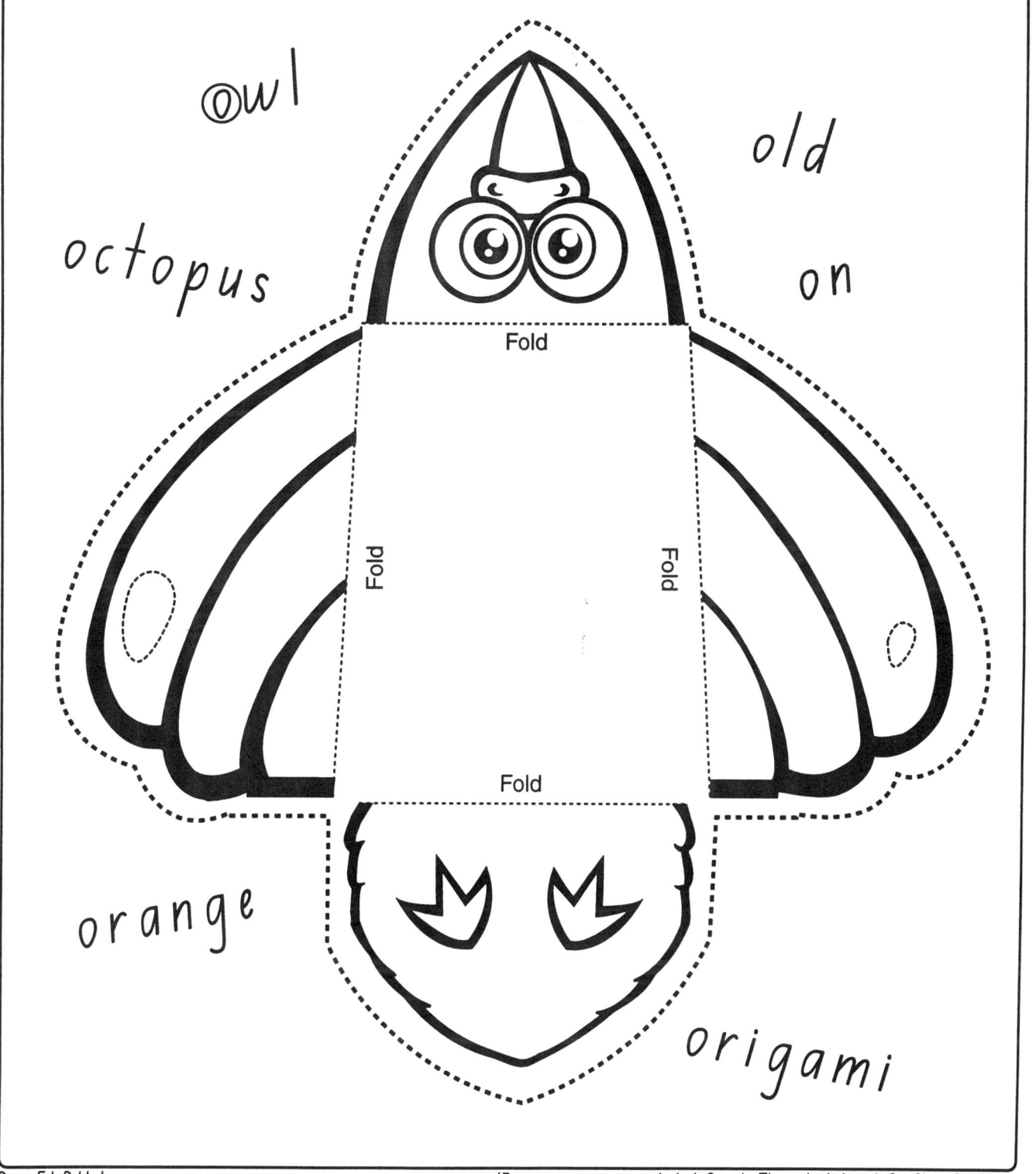

owl

old

octopus

on

Fold

Fold

Fold

Fold

orange

origami

Prim-Ed Publishing15Initial Sounds Through Art and Craft — Book 2

Pp is for parrot puppet

Instructions

1. Trace all the dotted letters.
2. Find and circle the initial sound in each word.
3. Colour then cut out the parrot.
4. Glue on feathers if available.
5. Carefully cut out the finger holes.

ⓟet

panda

parrot

pirate

pat

pig

puppet

pelican

Prim-Ed Publishing — 16 — Initial Sounds Through Art and Craft – Book 2

Qq is for quiet queen

Instructions

1. Trace all the dotted letters.
2. Find and circle the initial sound in each word.
3. Colour and cut out the queen, her clothes and crown.
4. Dress her up and walk her along.

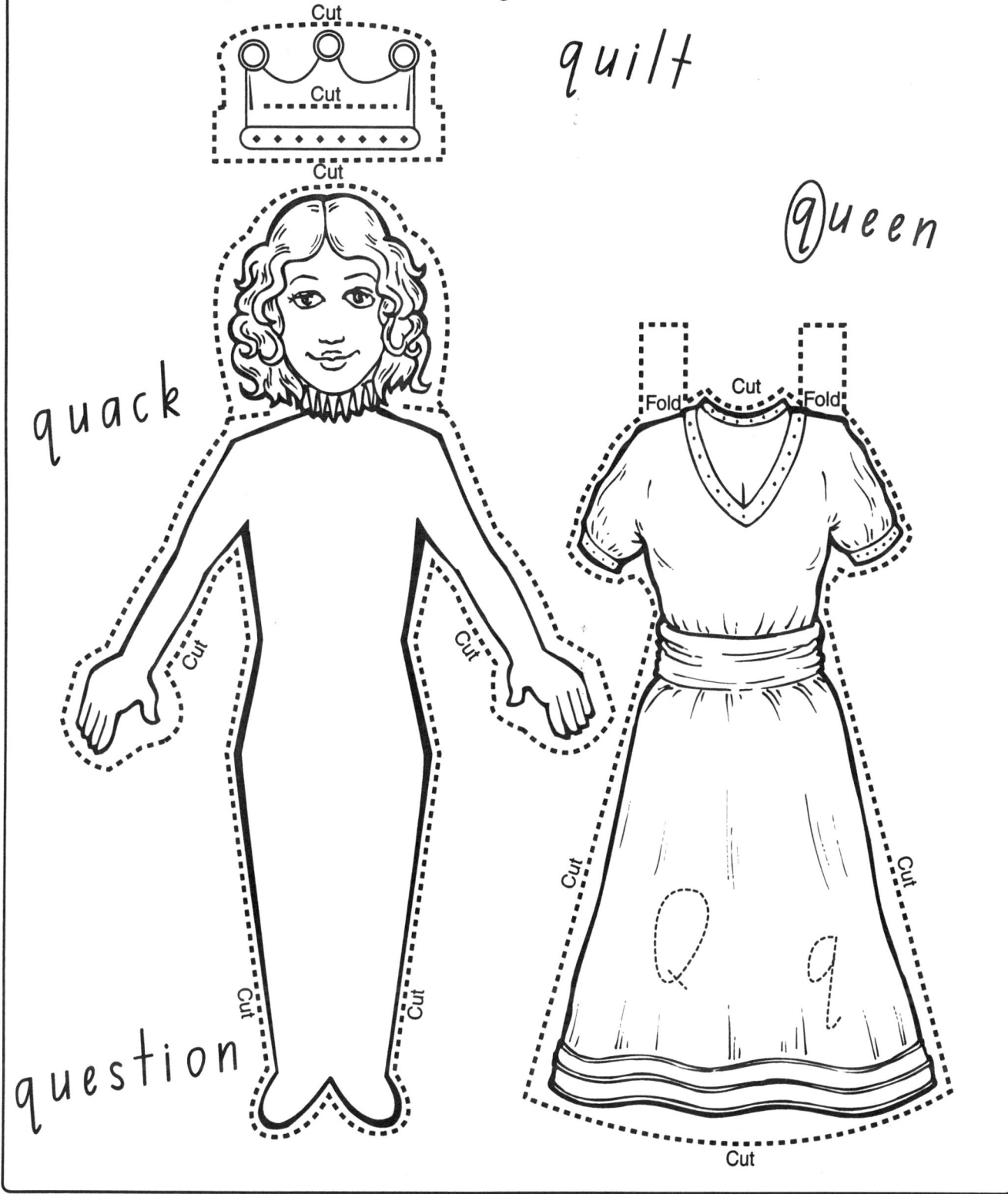

quilt

ⓠueen

quack

question

Rr is for Ralph Rooster

Instructions

1. Trace all the dotted letters.
2. Find and circle the initial sound in each word.
3. Colour and cut out the rooster and the wheel.
4. Cut out the dotted area on the wheel.
5. Attach wheel to rooster with a split pin.
6. Spin wheel to find the letters.

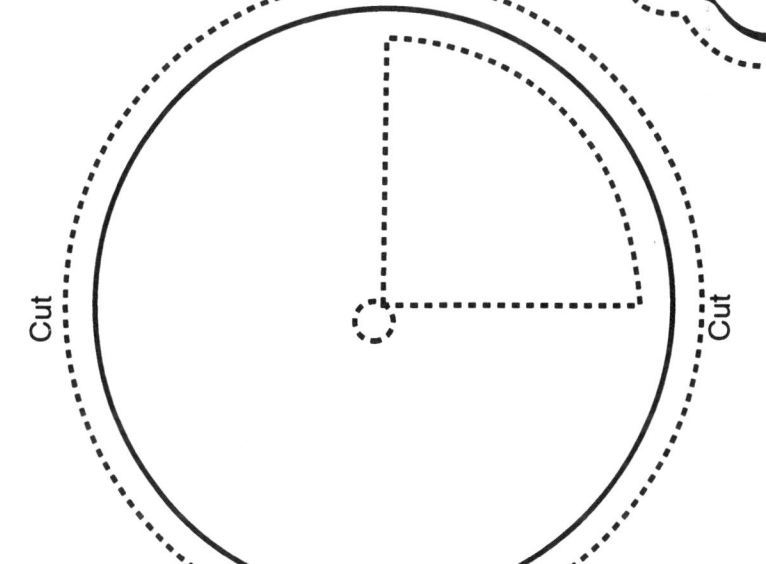

red

rabbit

rooster

robot

Prim-Ed Publishing — Initial Sounds Through Art and Craft — Book 2

Ss is for silver star

Instructions

1. Trace all the dotted letters.
2. Find and circle the initial sound in each word.
3. Colour and cut out the star.
4. Put silver glitter on the points of the star.
5. Attach string.

silver

spider

snail

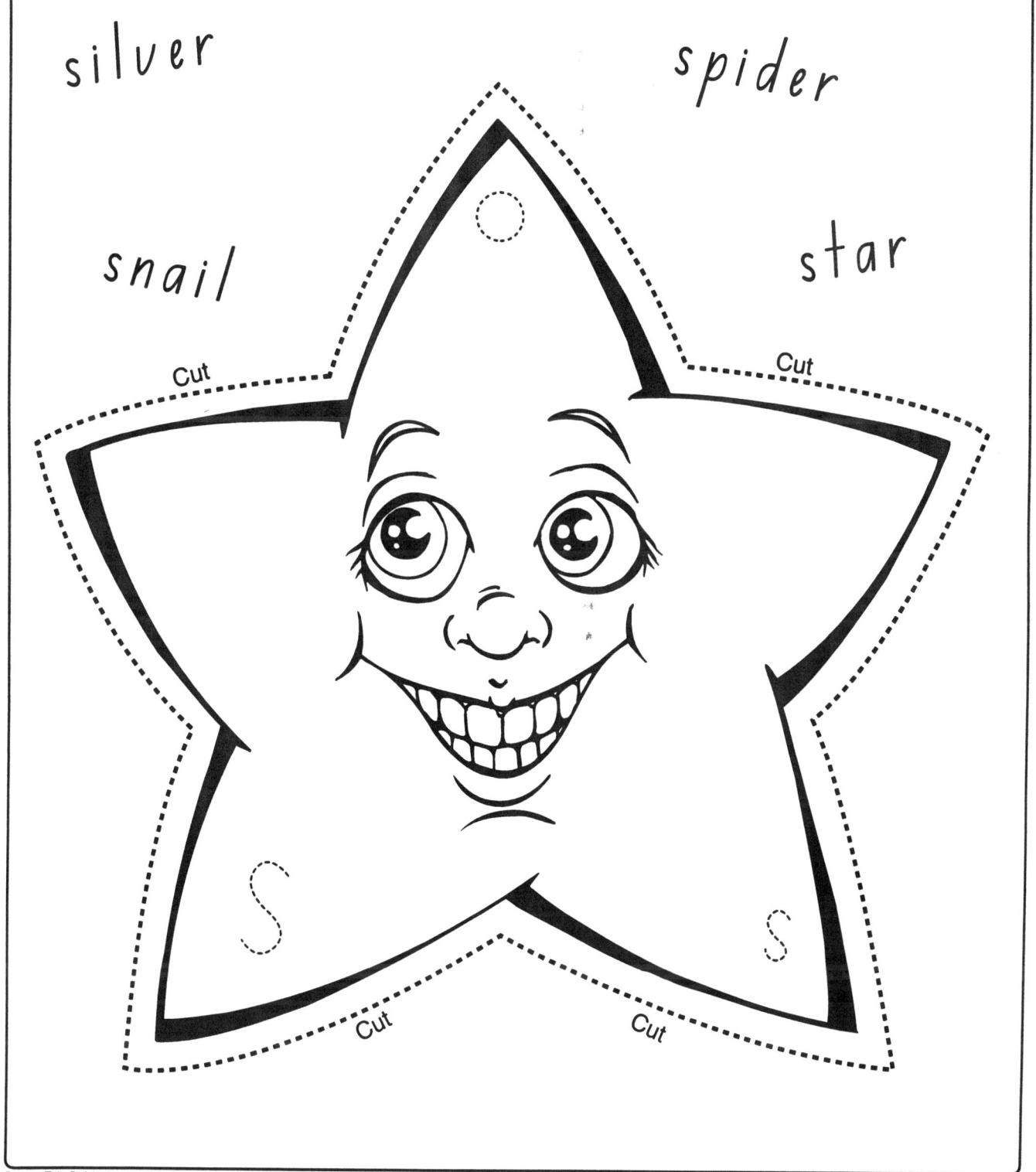

star

Tt is for Timothy Tiger

Instructions

1. Trace all the dotted letters.
2. Find and circle the initial sound in each word.
3. Colour and cut out the mask.
4. Attach pipe-cleaner whiskers.
5. Carefully cut out eye holes.
6. Attach string to the sides.

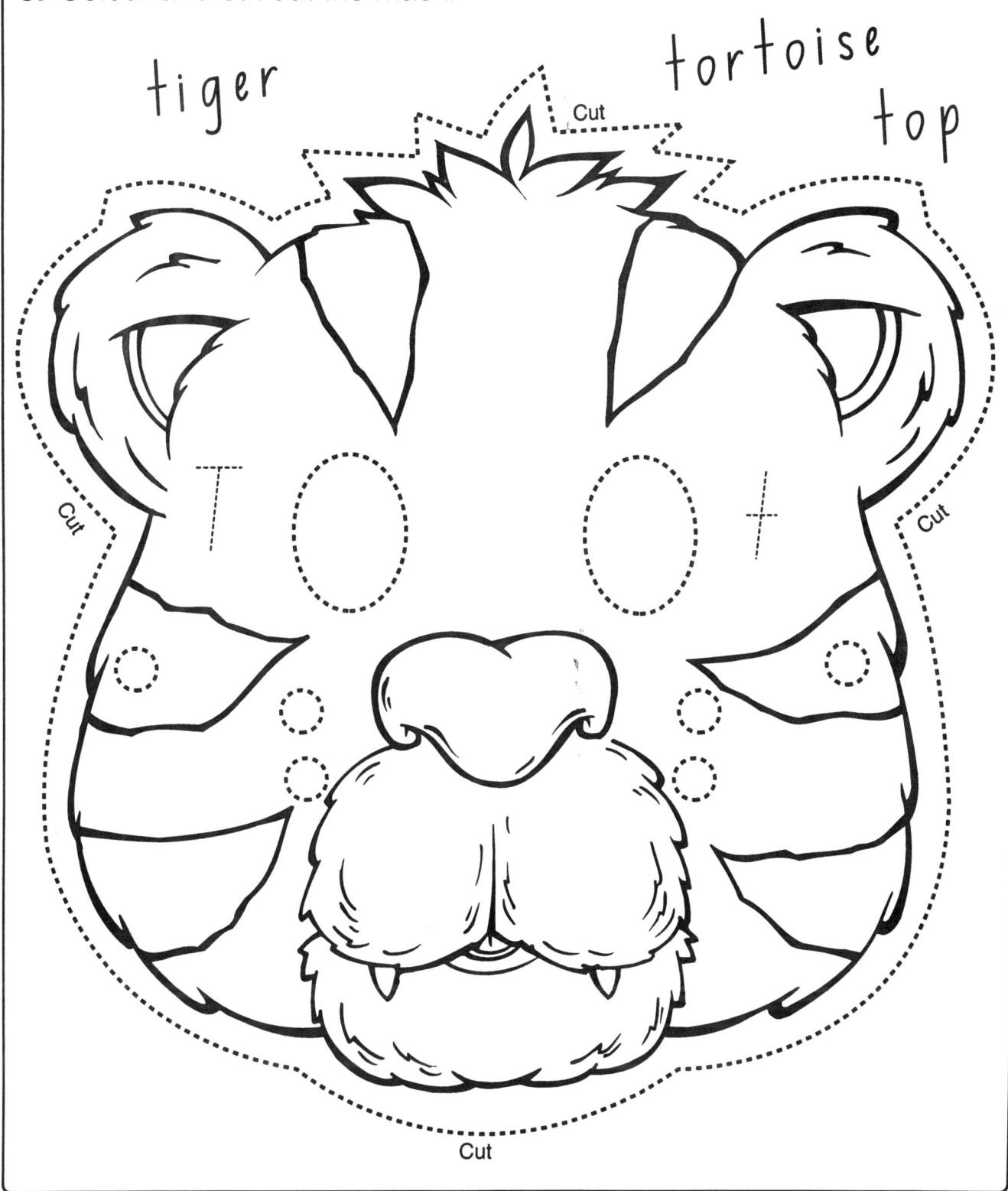

tiger

tortoise

top

Cut

Uu is for stand-up U

Instructions

1. Trace all the dotted letters.
2. Find and circle the initial sound in each word.
3. Cut out the rectangle.
4. Fold over and cut out stand-up U.
5. Stand it up.

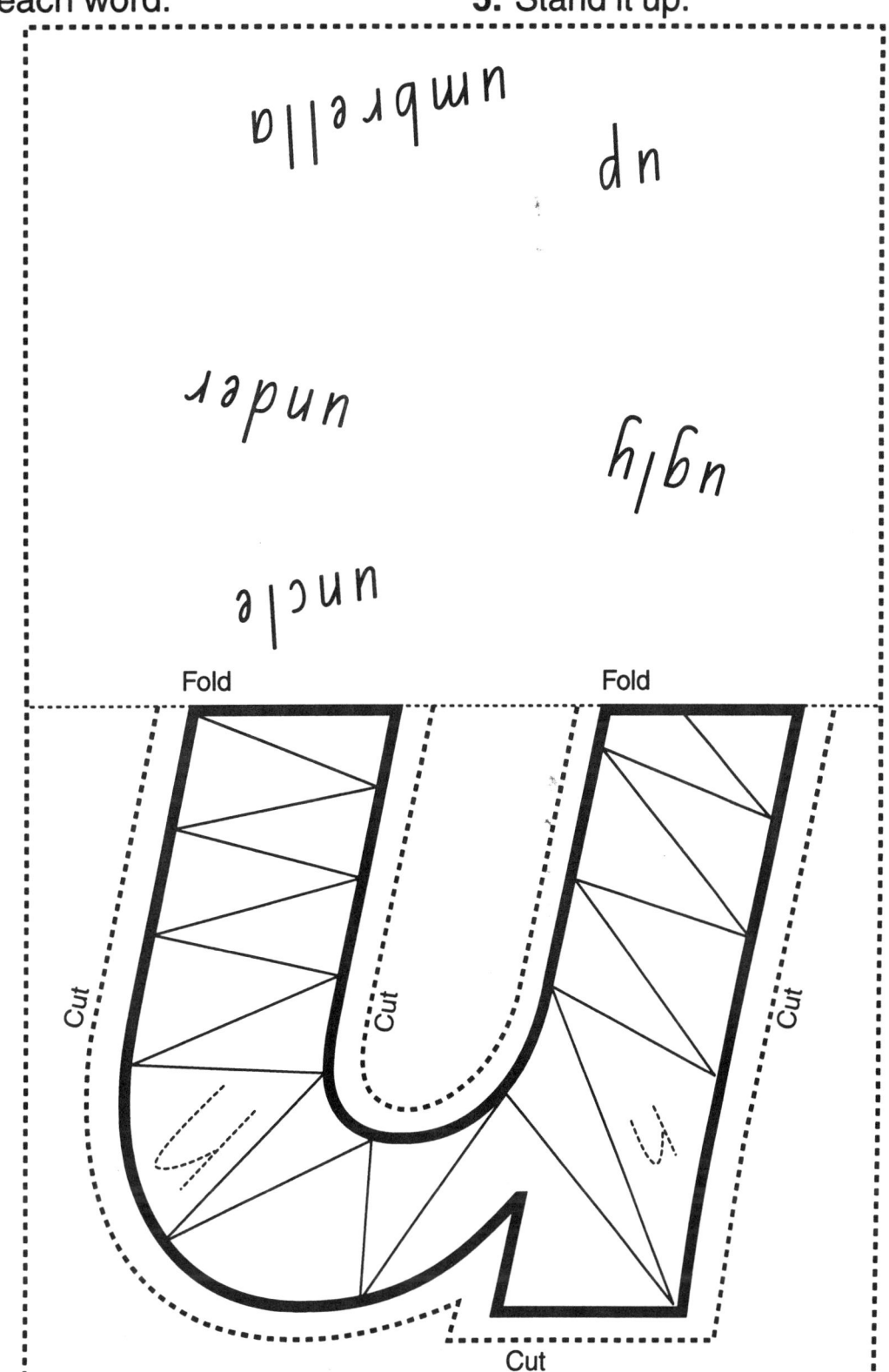

umbrella

up

under

ugly

uncle

Fold   Fold

Cut   Cut   Cut

Cut

Vv is for Victor Vegetable

Instructions

1. Trace over the dotted letters.
2. Find and circle the initial sound in each word.
3. Colour and cut out all the vegetables.
4. Glue them together to make your own vegetable man called Victor.

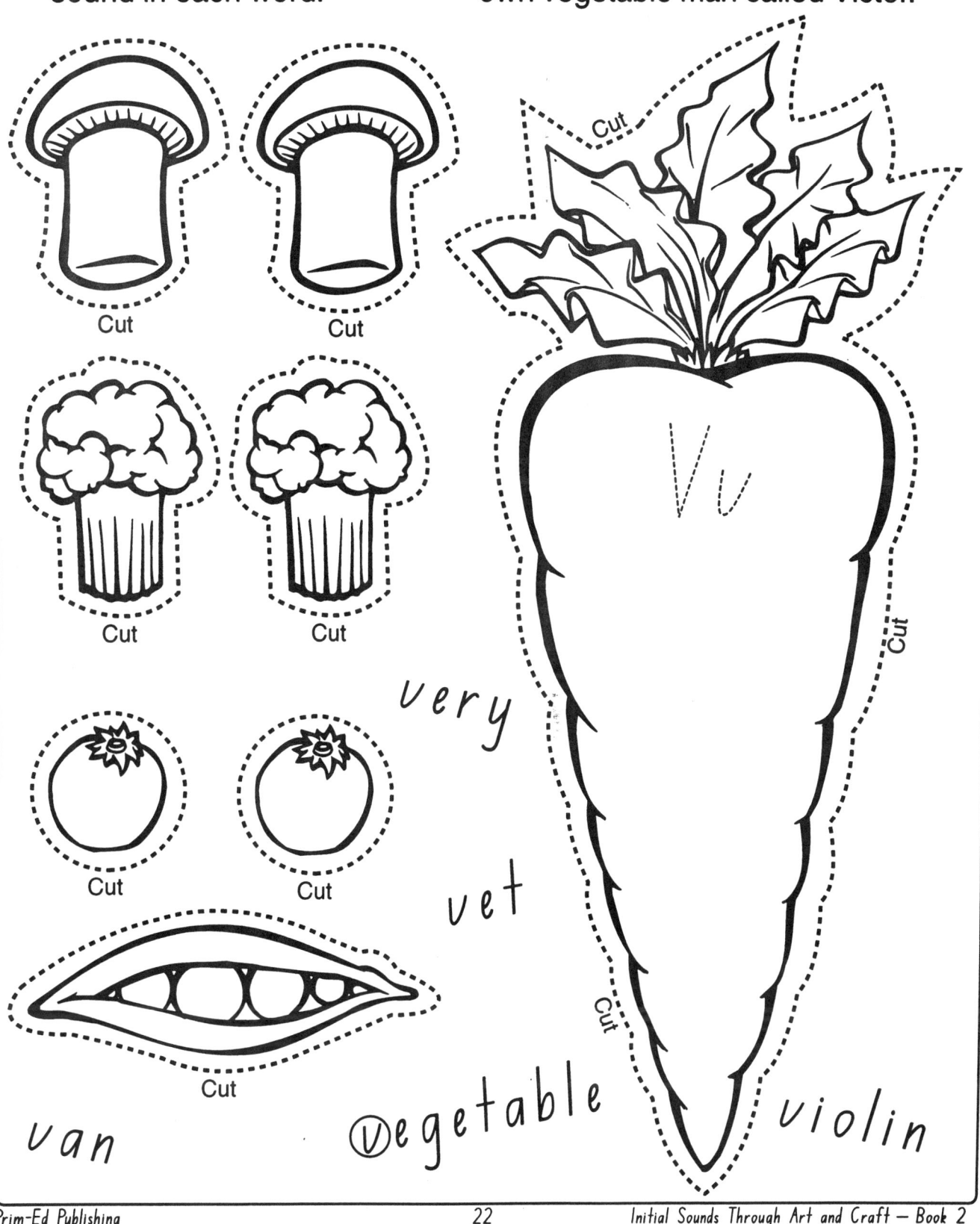

very

vet

van ⓥegetable violin

Prim-Ed Publishing 22 Initial Sounds Through Art and Craft — Book 2

Ww is for wacky weather wheel

Instructions

1. Trace all the dotted letters.
2. Find and circle the initial sound in each word.
3. Colour all the weather pictures.
4. Cut out wheels and glue back-to-back.
5. Punch a hole in the middle.
6. Fold a piece of string in half and thread through the holes in the middle of the wheel.
7. Tie ends of string. Place fingers in each end and pull. This makes the wheel spin.

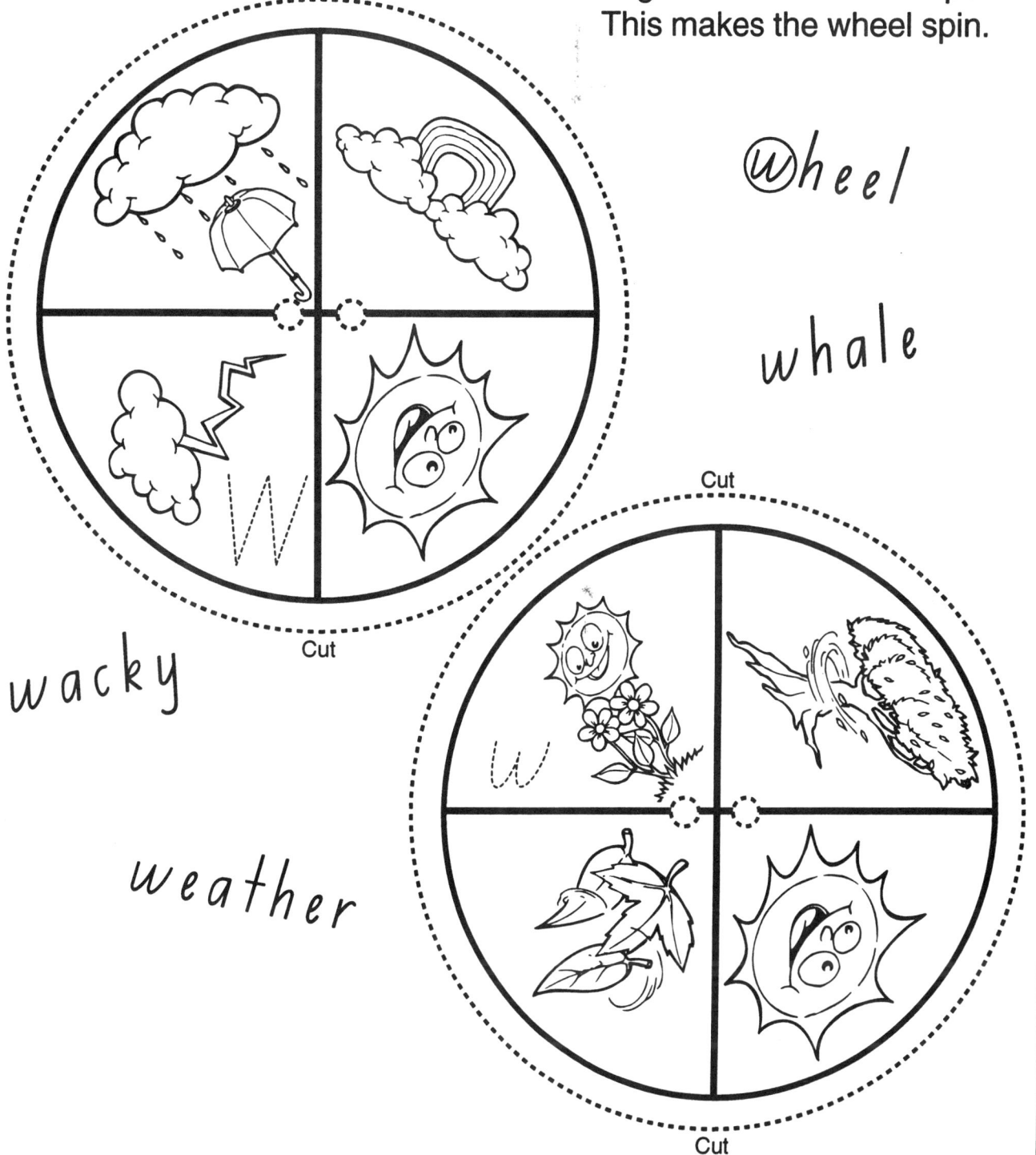

ⓦheel

whale

wacky

weather

Prim-Ed Publishing   23   Initial Sounds Through Art and Craft – Book 2

Xx is for X-ray Max

Instructions

1. Trace all the dotted letters.
2. Find and circle the initial sound in each word.
3. Colour and cut out Max.
4. Colour and cut out the x-ray.
5. Fold the tabs of the x-ray and place on Max.

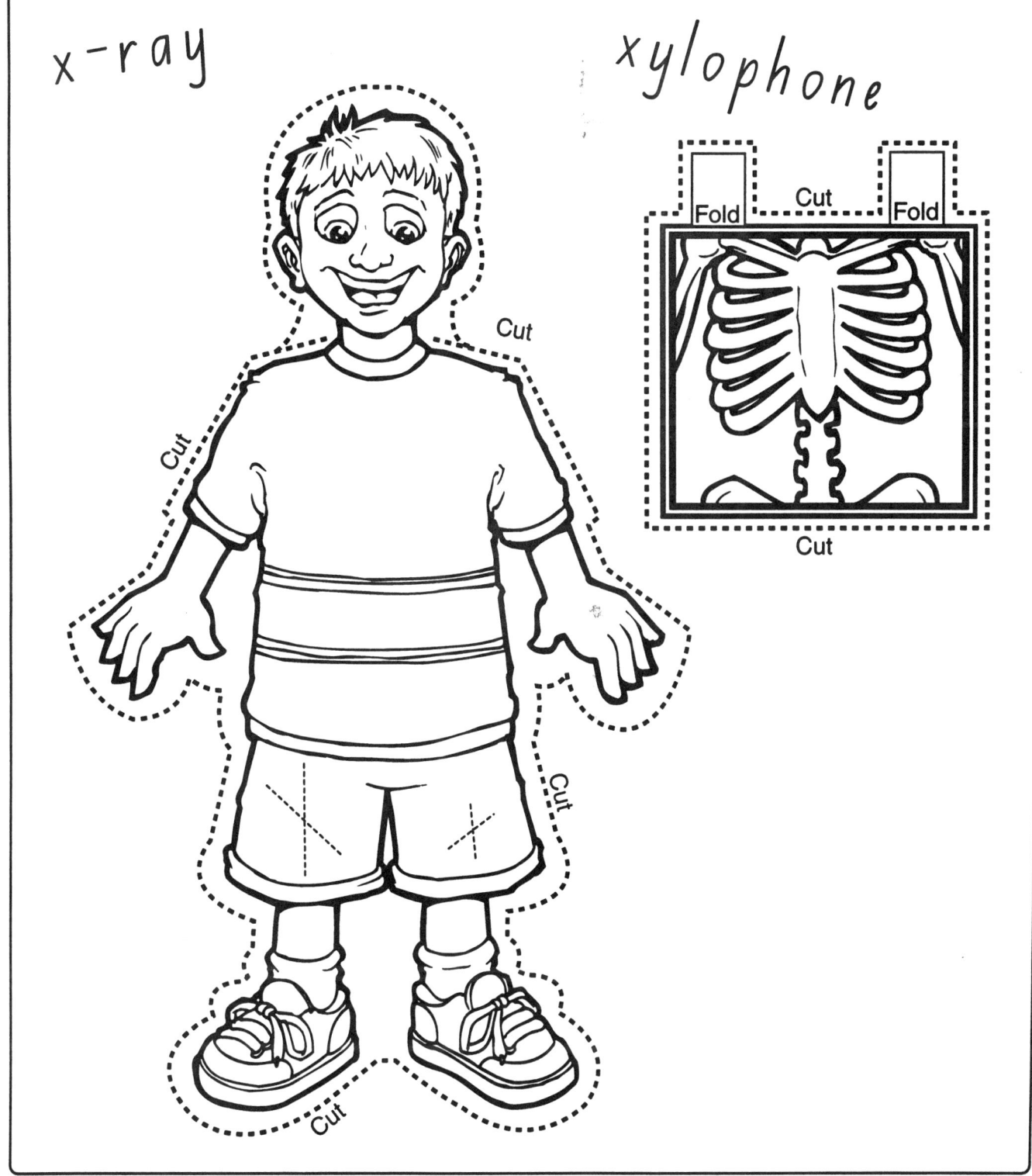

x-ray

xylophone

Fold Cut Fold

Cut

Cut

Cut

Cut

Prim-Ed Publishing

Initial Sounds Through Art and Craft — Book 2

Yy is for yellow yacht

Instructions

1. Trace all the dotted letters.
2. Find and circle the initial sound in each word.
3. Colour the water and the yacht.
4. Cut out the rectangle.
5. Cut out the dotted shapes.
6. Glue yellow cellophane across the back of the picture.

yacht   yes   yellow

Prim-Ed Publishing   25   Initial Sounds Through Art and Craft – Book 2

Zz Zelda Zebra at the zoo

Instructions

1. Trace all the dotted letters.
2. Find and circle the initial sound in each word.
3. Cut out Zelda and the shapes.
4. Glue the shapes correctly on Zelda.
5. Colour Zelda.

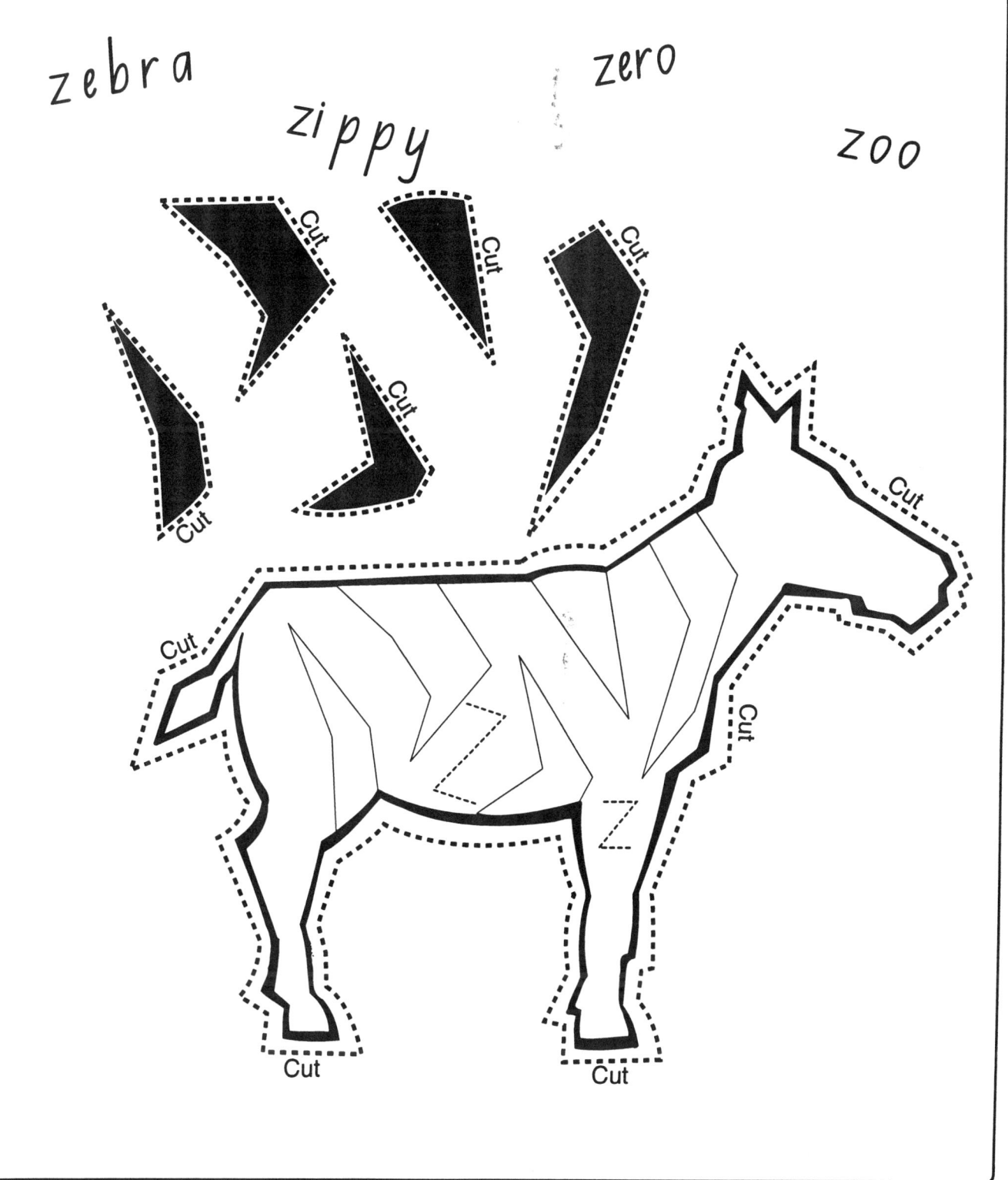

zebra

zippy

zero

zoo